- STRATEGIES FOR -
KINGDOM DOMINION

A 21-Day Journey to Accessing the Many
Privileges of Being a Kingdom Citizen

TOKONI CHERYLE BUSH

Tokoni
CHERYLE BUSH
MINISTRIES
"Empowering People, Changing lives, Impacting Nations"

Strategies for Kingdom Dominion: A 21-Day Journey to Accessing the Many Privileges of Being a Kingdom Citizen

Tokoni Cheryle Bush Ministries
www.tcbministries.org

Book Creation and Design
DHBonner Virtual Solutions, LLC
www.dhbonner.net

ISBN: 978-0-578-70576-7

Printed in the United States of America

This book is dedicated to Nancy Tubman Reese, the woman who taught me the foundational basics of prayer. Apostle Nancy, *thank you* for the valuable lessons I am still applying to my life. May the Lord richly and immensely bless you for the many wisdom nuggets and prayer principles you have sown into my life. *You are a true mother in Zion.*

Table of Contents

Foreword

> "And God blessed them, and God said unto them, Be fruitful, and multiply, and replenish the earth, and subdue it: and have dominion over the fish of the sea, and over the fowl of the air, and over every living thing that moveth upon the earth." -Genesis 1:28

Strategies for Kingdom Dominion is a daily devotional that has been researched skillfully to enable us to appropriate the supernatural for unlimited possibilities. This is one of the best devotionals, written by an inspired mind. I am hoping that as you sit with God alone for the period stated, you will find your place in the kingdom using these strategies.

> "For the earnest expectation of the creature waiteth for the manifestation of the sons of God."
> -Romans 8:19

It is a privilege to write the foreword for this book and extend the kingdom, giving the next generations their portion. Tokoni Cheryle Bush, an Apostle with the fivefold ministerial mantles, brings the truth of strategies for kingdom dominion in the pages of this devotional. Therefore, read with an expectation as God commanded Joshua in Joshua 1:8: "This book of the law shall not depart out of thy mouth; but thou shalt meditate therein day and night, that thou mayest observe to do according to all that is written therein; for then thou shalt make thy way prosperous, and then thou shalt have good success."

Remember, God made you in His image — as a co-creator — with a dominion mandate, and will find your position with persecution, perseverance, and promotion to the place of Glory and Honor.

"For thou hast made him a little lower than the angels, and hast crowned him with glory and honour. Thou madest him to have dominion over the works of thy hands; thou hast put all things under his feet: All sheep and oxen, yea, and the beasts of the field; The fowl of the air, and the fish of the sea, and whatsoever passeth through the paths of the seas. O LORD our Lord, how excellent is thy name in all the earth!"

-Psalm 8:5-9

Dr. Tam Seth Eyedoude
Senior Pastor, *The Redeemed Glory Family Church*
Bayelsa State, Nigeria

Introduction

This journal is the result of many failures, disappointments, and cycles of regret. I have learned through trial and error the significance of knowing who you are and whose you are. Too many kingdom citizens are living beneath their kingdom privileges, which has debilitated our growth, stagnated our momentum, and robbed many of the ability to hope in the Lord. It is past time that we position ourselves — not according to our past, gender, or racial limitations — but according to the Word of God. It is time for us to walk in the power and authority that we were predestined to possess.

Join me on a 21-day journey to a renewed perspective, limitless possibilities, and great success, where each day, you will have a Scripture to read, a journal assignment, and a prayer to declare. May the reading and implementation of the strategies provided unlock new places of influence, mantle you with overwhelming victorious living, and create a hunger for what already belongs to you.

Father, anoint this reader to not just read, but to comprehend what the Spirit of the Lord is saying to them. I pray that You stretch their expectations and desires for the manifestation of the kingdom citizen You have predestined to come forth at this present time. May Your name alone be magnified and glorified, and the kingdoms of this world be dismantled and repositioned in the reader's heart and mind — in the Holy and Majestic name of our precious Savior, Jesus Christ.

Amen.

Inquire of the Lord

"And David enquired at the Lord, saying, Shall I pursue after this troop? shall I overtake them? And he answered him, Pursue: for thou shalt surely overtake them, and without fail recover all." –1 Samuel 30:8

If we are ever to experience the freedom and liberty that God has preordained for us as heirs of His kingdom, we must learn to inquire of the Lord. David conquered many giants (seemingly impossible situations) with one strategy. And David inquired of the Lord. 2 Samuel 5:19, 1 Samuel 30:8 and 1 Samuel 23:2 all begin with the wise decision of David that brought forth awesome victory on his behalf.

David learned that if he had the Lord's stamp of approval, all would be well. Many times, we enter battles ill-equipped. What soldier attempts to implement a plan without prior consent from his commanding officer?

Oftentimes, we see a battle and decide to join in without prior knowledge of the desired outcome, the consequences, or if we are on the list of required participants. I am merely saying seek God first! Know if He is calling you to war or rest in Him, Weigh the consequences and find out if there are any spoils (rewards) involved.

JOURNAL ASSIGNMENT: List a few situations where you neglected to inquire of the Lord before making decisions or reacting. Were there favorable results? Or, are you still paying for the consequences?

_____

_____

_____

_____

_____

_____

_____

_____

_____

_____

_____

_____

_____

_____

_____

_____

_____

_____

_____

_____

_____

_____

_____

_____

_____

_____

_____

_____

_____

_____

_____

_____

_____

_____

IMPLEMENTATION: Come up with a plan regarding future decisions.

PRAYER

God, I do not want to be before You, nor do I want to be behind You. I want to be divinely aligned with Your will for my life. Teach me Your timing. I desire the anointing of the sons of Issachar. Teach me to discern my seasons and timing so that I may effectively implement kingdom principles in the earth realm. Teach me to come to You before I make decisions. Show me how to wait on You before I move. In Jesus' name, Amen.

Day 02

Do Not Judge

"Judge not, that ye be not judged. For with what judgment ye judge, ye shall be judged: and with what measure ye mete, it shall be measured to you again. And why beholdest thou the mote that is in thy brother's eye, but considerest not the beam that is in thine own eye? Or how wilt thou say to thy brother, Let me pull out the mote out of thine eye; and, behold, a beam is in thine own eye? Thou hypocrite, first cast out the beam out of thine own eye; and then shalt thou see clearly to cast out the mote out of thy brother's eye." –Matthew 7:1-5

It is so easy to judge your sister or brother if you have not been where they are or gone through what they have. I believe God is calling us to pray more and talk less.

James 1:19 states: "Wherefore, my beloved brethren, let every man be swift to hear, slow to speak, slow to wrath:"

In this time of great temptation, it does not surprise me that many are finding themselves in situations that do not represent the kingdom well. I am sure you can recall a circumstance or two where you needed the compassion, love, and support of others. We must purpose in our hearts to show forth the forgiving compassion of Christ. Remember, no matter what they did, Christ died for that sin. We diminish the power of Jesus' resurrection every time we judge.

JOURNAL ASSIGNMENT: Write down the people you have judged unfairly (not according to the Word of God) and then write out a proper response to their actions or deeds.

_____

_____

_____

_____

_____

_____

_____

_____

_____

_____

_____

_____

_____

_____

_____

_____

_____

_____

_____

_____

_____

_____

_____

_____

_____

_____

_____

_____

_____

_____

_____

IMPLEMENTATION: Make a conscious decision to live a Judgment-free life.

PRAYER

Father God, I decree and declare that I am a conduit of Your love. Just as Your love flows to me, it flows through me. I impact many lives by the way I love. I have the eyes of God. I see past faults and tap into the need for love and the need for compassion. I declare that I will not only talk of my love, but I will also show it. I will pray more and talk less. In Jesus' name, Amen.

Day 03

You Must Maintain a Forward Momentum

"Brethren, I count not myself to have apprehended: but this one thing I do, forgetting those things which are behind, and reaching forth unto those things which are before, I press toward the mark for the prize of the high calling of God in Christ Jesus. Let us therefore, as many as be perfect, be thus minded: and if in anything ye be otherwise minded, God shall reveal even this unto you. Nevertheless, whereto we have already attained, let us walk by the same rule, let us mind the same thing. Brethren be followers together of me and mark them which walk so as ye have us for an example. (For many walk, of whom I have told you often, and now tell you even weeping, that they are the enemies of the cross of Christ: Whose end is destruction, whose God is their belly, and whose glory is in their shame, who mind earthly things.)"

—Philippians 3:13-19

The key to success in this hour is momentum! Everybody starts off excited. It is not how you start that matters but your ability to remain consistent, dedicated, and faithful through the duration of the assignment. Kingdom assignments are challenged because the adversary to the manifestation of the promise will do whatever is needed to cause you to abort the mission.

You must remain vigilant concerning those things you have been assigned, in order to reap the harvest of manifestation. Purpose in your heart to press past and through any level of opposition to the will of the Lord concerning your life.

Jesus was so vigilant about His purpose that He addressed the enemy in Peter in Matthew 16:23. He recognized that Peter (although his motive was pure) had the potential to cause Him to abort His mission.

JOURNAL ASSIGNMENT: Write down the things/people that you know have the potential to stop or distract you from your kingdom momentum. Strategize on how you will avoid or diminish the authority you have given them.

_____

_____

_____

_____

_____

_____

_____

_____

_____

_____

_____

_____

_____

_____

_____

_____

_____

_____

_____

_____

IMPLEMENTATION: Write declarations regarding your kingdom momentum, the value of being consistent, and any future hindrances.

PRAYER

As you face this day, I pray a world-overcoming ability to advance over you! I declare that regardless of the circumstances, you will go forward. I decree that your momentum concerning the things of God increases! I declare that you will not look to the left or right but unto the hills toward your great and mighty Helper! This is your season of advancement! Advancement in your relationships. Advancement in your home. Advancement on your job. Advancement now, in the name of Jesus!

Day 04

Let Nothing Frustrate Your Wait!

> "I had fainted, unless I had believed to see the goodness of the Lord in the land of the living. Wait on the Lord: be of good courage, and he shall strengthen thine heart: wait, I say, on the Lord." —Psalms 27:13-14

There is something about waiting that we have all had a problem with at some point! We live in a microwave society that teaches us that we must have everything *now!* Therefore, when we find ourselves in our *wait season,* we quickly become frustrated and begin to complain. Isaiah 40:31 (MSG) reads:

> "But those who wait upon God get fresh strength. They spread their wings and soar like eagles, they run and do not get tired, they walk and do not lag behind."

So, there you have it! The waiting process develops a level of perseverance and press that far exceeds that of many others.

There is something about you that has made the enemy so incredibly uncomfortable. He has glimpsed the extraordinary level of breakthrough and overcome that you are about to experience, so he is trying to frustrate your wait — but not so! I do not know about you, but I have come too far! We are too close! Nothing and nobody will frustrate my "wait"! Come on and say this out of your mouth:

> "I will wait on the lord. I won't go before Him, and I cannot afford to be behind Him. My steps are ordered by Him, and I will wait on Him, in Jesus' name!"

JOURNAL ASSIGNMENT: In what areas are you struggling with waiting on the Lord? Confront them and write out your plan to counteract the feelings and emotions associated.

_____

_____

_____

_____

_____

_____

_____

_____

_____

_____

_____

_____

_____

_____

_____

_____

_____

_____

_____

_____

_____

IMPLEMENTATION: Write Declarations regarding your struggles, find Scriptures, and meditate on them throughout the day.

PRAYER

Father, I struggle with waiting on You. Life has taught me to make things happen. However, Your Word encourages me to wait. Sometimes, I become frustrated, and this causes me to move before I should. Show me how to trust You. Increase my patience; I greatly desire to see Your will manifested in my life. In Jesus' name. Amen.

Day 05

Walk in Your Authority

"And these signs shall follow them that believe; In my name shall they cast out devils; they shall speak with new tongues; They shall take up serpents; and if they drink any deadly thing, it shall not hurt them; they shall lay hands on the sick, and they shall recover." —Mark 16:17-18

efore Jesus left this earth, we were given a mandate as believers. We have already been empowered with a level of power and authority that will thoroughly protect, cover, and keep us. Often, as believers, we fail to walk in the level of authority that we have and, instead, live unfulfilled lives, leaving un-walked out destinies and Purpose.

It is time to embrace the Authority that you have been given and show forth the works of Jesus in the Earth Realm! Make a conscious decision today to be and do Jesus on earth. It is time to reign in the earth as we already do in heaven.

JOURNAL ASSIGNMENT: Write your declaration and find Scriptures regarding your kingdom authority.

_____

_____

_____

_____

_____

_____

_____

_____

_____

_____

IMPLEMENTATION: Meditate on the Scriptures in your journal throughout the day.

PRAYER

Father, today, I acknowledge Your power, and I make a stance in my kingdom authority! I walk in kingdom confidence, and I declare and decree breakthrough, miracles, provision, and overflow for this day. I expect the authority of the kingdom to manifest blessings, healing, and deliverance wherever You send me this day and many days to follow! Hallelujah! I receive and decree it NOW! In the name of Jesus, Amen.

Day 06

Take the Limits Off!

> "For My thoughts are not your thoughts, neither are your ways My ways, says the Lord. For as the heavens are higher than the earth, so are My ways higher than your ways and My thoughts than your thoughts." —Isaiah 55:8-9

*G*ood Morning! *Open doors* are awaiting your arrival! What are you waiting for? God desires to show Himself strong and mighty in the lives of His ppl. No time to waste.

Embrace the limitless opportunities available to you as an heir of the kingdom. I do not know about you, but for me, it is up from here. You are anointed to surpass limitations. God desires that we live limitless lives, have unlimited mindsets, and tap into Him — the God of possibility! So, take the limits off and SOAR!

Take the limits off what you are expecting in this season! We have often heard, "Think outside the box!" Today I encourage you to expect outside the box!

No matter what the situation is, how impossible it looks, or how hard it gets, I want you to remember that you serve a God of limitless possibilities. He is working it out, and you will come out of this, not looking or feeling like what you have been through. God sees and knows.

It is not about what they said, or they think. The Word of God concerning your life is the only thing that matters! I declare today that you are coming out of the limitations that have been put on you by man. You will transcend every limitation on your life. Here is to limitless living!

JOURNAL ASSIGNMENT: In what areas have you been living in the constraints of other's opinions? In what areas have you been constrained by what society has dictated? Write out a positive declaration regarding your new life of limitless possibilities.

_____

_____

_____

_____

_____

_____

_____

_____

_____

_____

_____

_____

_____

_____

_____

_____

_____

_____

_____

_____

_____

_____

_____

_____

_____

_____

_____

IMPLEMENTATION: Find Scriptures regarding limitless living and meditate on them throughout the day.

PRAYER

Father, we declare today that we are taking the limits off! That we are embracing every assignment with victory in mind. We are no longer held captive by the past, what somebody else could not do, or others' inability to see us victorious. We declare today that we are coming out of generational, spiritual, physical, financial, and mental limitations. We are soaring! In the name of Jesus, Amen.

Day 07

Know Your God!

> "...but the people that do know their God shall be strong, and do exploits." —Daniel 11:32b

In order to effectively administrate the kingdom dominion that you have been given, you must know your God! It is so much easier to face difficult situations when you know whose you are. David faced Goliath, the giant (a seemingly impossible situation) with great confidence because he knew who he was. His response to adversity was (1 Samuel 17:34-36):

> "And David said unto Saul, "Thy servant kept his father's sheep, and there came a lion, and a bear, and took a lamb out of the flock: And I went out after him, and smote him, and delivered it out of his mouth: and when he arose against me, I caught him by his beard, and smote him, and slew him. Thy servant slew both the lion and the bear: and this uncircumcised Philistine shall be as one of them, seeing he hath defied the armies of the living God."

David knew he had a blood-bought right to victory. He knew the track record of His God was flawless, and this empowered him to conquer the lion and the bear. When you are confident in God's ability, nothing can stop, detour, or derail you!

No matter what your situation says, the voice of God (the Word of God) should be louder and clearer. I would like to challenge you to purposely spend time with the Lord, pray in the Holy Ghost, and allow Him to build you up in Him. God desires to show Himself strong in the earth realm through you!

JOURNAL ASSIGNMENT: In what areas have you had a lower perspective of yourself? In what ways have these views debilitated you? Write a positive affirmation about who you are in Christ.

_____

_____

_____

_____

_____

_____

_____

_____

_____

_____

_____

_____

_____

_____

_____

_____

_____

_____

_____

_____

_____

_____

_____

_____

IMPLEMENTATION: Read your affirmation aloud seven times today.

PRAYER

Father, I thank You that You are ruling in the earth through me. Continue to strengthen my ability to rely on You. Continue to show me how to trust Your ability to show yourself strong in every situation in my life. My faith is aligned with Your Word. My confidence is aligned with Your Word! My life is aligned with Your Word! In Jesus' name. Amen.

Day 08

Embrace the Chosen Path for Your Life!

> "And he was withdrawn from them about a stone's cast, and kneeled down, and prayed, Saying, Father, if thou be willing, remove this cup from me: nevertheless not my will, but thine, be done." —Luke 22:41-42

Chosen is derived from the word "choose." It means selected: picked out from or preferred to the rest—one who, or that which is the object of choice or special favor. So, I guess it is safe to safe to say that if you are chosen, you have been hand-selected or favored immensely by God!

The chosen hear or are sensitive to the call of God. The chosen are rooted and grounded in God! They have an unrelenting, never-ceasing connection with God that cannot be interrupted by man. They are hooked-up, tied up, and tangled up in Jesus.

They do not hear anyone but God and what He is saying because that is what is critical in this hour. They have made a conscious decision to transcend the limitations, boldly embrace the fullness of what has been stored up for them by Father, and to live a life that is pleasing — not to man — but to God.

I genuinely believe that a clarion call has been released, and God is preparing a people that will lay aside any and everything that is required to do the will of the one that has sent them.

JOURNAL ASSIGNMENT: Write Scriptures regarding embracing the will of the Lord for your life.

_____

_____

_____

_____

_____

_____

_____

_____

_____

_____

_____

_____

_____

_____

_____

_____

_____

_____

_____

_____

_____

_____

_____

_____

_____

_____

_____

_____

_____

_____

_____

_____

IMPLEMENTATION: Meditate on the Scriptures throughout the day.

PRAYER

Father, I pray for your chosen today! I decree that they are positioning themselves to hear and implement kingdom at the pace you have called them to in this hour of their lives. I bind compromise off their lives. I declare a shift in their minds and hearts in this hour. As You are drawing them closer to You, I decree that they will answer and submit. Give them wisdom to create time and space for You in their daily schedules. Show them how to put You first, in the name of Jesus!

Day 09

Rest

> "For he who has once entered [God's] rest also has ceased from [the weariness and pain] of human labors, just as God rested from those labors [a]peculiarly His own."
> —Hebrews 4:10 AMP

Rest is a decision, mindset, and a place of confidence in God's Word. Rest is just that (not trying to make something happen, figure out a plan or solution). It comes when you surrender to God's plan and purpose for your life. It manifests when you truly *let go and let God.*

Rest is your way of saying, "God, I trust You. I trust your plan. I may not like or even understand the season I am in, but I will rest in the vastness of who You are." Rest comes when you finally decide to surrender your control to God. So, I encourage you to rest from this day forth. Have a supernaturally phenomenal day!

JOURNAL ASSIGNMENT: Find Scriptures regarding resting in God's plan and purpose for your life. Write out a declaration with the Scriptures.

_____

_____

_____

_____

_____

_____

_____

_____

_____

_____

_____

_____

_____

_____

IMPLEMENTATION: Say your declaration seven times today.

PRAYER

Father, teach me to embrace vulnerability. I can let my guard down with You because You have my best interest at heart. Teach me how to flow from this new place. Teach me how to truly lean, depend upon, and trust You. Show me the areas where I am fighting Your process. Fix anything that is not properly aligned with Your desire for my life in this season. I die, so that You may live through me.

Day 10

Stand!

So, my son, throw yourself into this work for Christ. Pass on what you heard from me-the whole congregation saying Amen! - to reliable leaders who are competent to teach others. When the going gets rough, take it on the chin with the rest of us, the way Jesus did. A soldier on duty does not get caught up in making deals at the marketplace. He concentrates on carrying out orders. An athlete who refuses to play by the rules will never get anywhere. It is the diligent farmer who gets the produce. Think it over. God will make it all plain. —2 Timothy 2:1-7 MSG

I *would like to encourage* you today to stand and having done all to stand, stand some more. Your God is not a God that lies or changes His mind. If He has spoken it, you can bank on it. You cannot afford to quit, throw in the towel, give up, or slow down in this hour. You literally must do what Paul, while in prison facing a death sentence, exhorted Timothy to do.

You will notice that Paul just broke it down. He said, grow up and take it like a man! Or, shall I say The Man (Jesus). In other words, Paul was showing us that everyone with great purpose and great destiny will have issues, frustrations, adversities, etc. However, we should not allow ourselves to have pity parties, woe is me sessions, or why is it so hard for me conferences!

We all face adverse times, and when in the midst, it seems as if we will never come out, but God shows up every time! He does not leave us hanging. Look at the last situation that God brought you out of. If He did it then, He will do it this time.

JOURNAL ASSIGNMENT: Write out the areas you are struggling in keeping focused, diligence, and being persistent. Write out your strategy for change.

_____

_____

_____

_____

_____

_____

_____

_____

_____

_____

_____

_____

_____

_____

_____

_____

IMPLEMENTATION: Write your declarations and find Scriptures regarding being steadfast and staying motivated and meditate on them throughout the day.

PRAYER

I decree a "Finisher's Anointing" over your life. From this day forward, you will complete every task that Father places before you. The Word quit will never be associated with you again. You will be known for the level of grace that is prominent over your life to do many things at one time in excellence that brings glory and reverence to the name of the Lord and the kingdom that is definitely tangible for you from this day forth.

You will run through troops and leap over walls for the glorification and edification of the Kingdom of God. Greatness is in your DNA, and that is what you shall produce from this day forward in the earth realm.

I declare today that you will not quit, run, throw in the towel, or abort the very purpose that you are carrying! You will stand and having done all to stand, stand still, and see the Salvation of the Lord! You will run and not be weary, and you will walk and not faint. You now operate in a new dimension of Kingdom momentum that is divinely connected to the heartbeat and will of the Father for your life... In Jesus' name!

Day 11

Dwell

> "He who dwells in the shelter of the Most High Will remain secure and rest in the shadow of the Almighty [whose power no enemy can withstand]. I will say of the LORD, "He is my refuge and my fortress, My God, in whom I trust [with great confidence, and on whom I rely]!'"
>
> —PSALMS 91:1-2 AMP

To *dwell means to* take up habitation, or to live or abide. When you purpose in your heart that you will do whatever it takes to dwell, live, abide or take up habitation in the presence of the Lord, you see, comprehend, and receive life's blows and disappointments differently.

If you hang around God long enough, you will begin to look, respond, and think like Him. You become a powerful force or tool against every enemy in your life.

Enoch dwelled at such a level that he no longer existed. You become who you spend the most time with. It is time to look, behave, and believe like God! Pursue and persistently dwell in the presence of the Lord!

JOURNAL ASSIGNMENT: What are the things that distract your consistent dwell? What has the potential to pull you from dwelling in the presence of the Lord? Develop a plan of persistent dwell.

_____

_____

_____

_____

_____

_____

_____

_____

_____

_____

_____

_____

_____

_____

_____

_____

_____

_____

_____

_____

_____

_____

_____

IMPLEMENTATION: Write your declaration, find Scriptures on dwelling in the presence of the Lord and meditate on them throughout the day.

PRAYER

Father, I decree that I am Your sheep and that I know Your voice. I will not follow the voice of a stranger, and I cut off every strange voice in my life. I declare that I am deaf to the voice of the enemy and every other voice contrary to Your will for my life. You are calling and wooing me in this hour, Father, and I will answer. I declare that I am not too busy to answer, but I hear Your call and quickly obey.

Remove any and everything in my heart that taints my ability to hear You clearly and accurately. I want to be divinely aligned with You in this hour as never before.

I truly desire to abide in the secret place so that I might partake of the secrets You are sharing. I need the instruction, revelation, and insight that only You can give. I desire a pure word from You for my situation and circumstances.

Yes, Lord, I will come higher! Draw me, and I will run after You. I will run fervently, passionately, and humbly to the high place in You, in the name of Jesus.

Day 12

Stop Expecting from Others What Only God Can Give!

> "...rendering service with goodwill, as to the Lord, and not [only] to men, knowing that whatever good thing each one does, he will receive this back from the Lord, whether [he is] slave or free." —Ephesians 6:7-8 AMP

W*e are to fear God* and *respect man*. However, this has not been the case in the lives of many. Frequently we fear man, which breeds a spirit of fear in many areas of our lives. This level of fear of rejection, fear of the repercussions of not doing everything right, and fear of man causes many God-ordained relationships to become tainted with hurt and offense.

Many run from place to place, looking for what only God can give. It is our responsibility to always point the people back to the Lord. The above passage assists in ensuring that things never get to this point. We are to be God-pleasers. We are to seek our affirmation from God. Many of us simply need to learn the depth of God's love toward us and embrace it. We expect too much from flesh; however, flesh will disappoint you every time because God will have no other gods before Him!

JOURNAL ASSIGNMENT: Do an honest assessment of yourself. What areas are you still seeking to please man? Are there undealt with issues that have caused you to have an unhealthy view of those in authority? Are there areas of rebellion in your heart because of unhealthy relationships?

_____

_____

_____

_____

_____

_____

_____

_____

_____

_____

_____

_____

_____

_____

_____

_____

_____

_____

_____

_____

_____

_____

_____

_____

_____

_____

_____

_____

_____

_____

_____

_____

IMPLEMENTATION: Write your declarations regarding healthy relationships, find Scriptures on pleasing God, and meditate on them throughout the day.

PRAYER:

Father, keep my heart and motives pure before You. I want to serve as unto You — not out of a need to be affirmed, validated, or loved. I desire to have a pure heart and motives concerning my kingdom connections. Dethrone every god in my life. Heal me of presumptuous behaviors directly connected to the rejection I have experienced in the past and equip me with the strength to endure this season — and those to come.

Find Your Tribe and Thrive

"And it came to pass, that, when Elisabeth heard the salutation of Mary, the babe leaped in her womb; and Elisabeth was filled with the Holy Ghost: And she spake out with a loud voice, and said, Blessed art thou among women, and blessed is the fruit of thy womb And whence is this to me, that the mother of my Lord should come to me? For, lo, as soon as the voice of thy salutation sounded in mine ears, the babe leaped in my womb for joy." —Luke 1:41-44

While on this thrive quest, you must purpose in your heart to surround yourself with people that see your potential and demand the fullness of it. The worst thing you can do is to relate to those who are comfortable with where you are. They will not demand the greater manifestation of the kingdom in your life. They like you right where you are because it does not cause them to change.

It is time to meet the Marys that have been predestined and ordained to cause your baby to leap! Not only did her baby leap, but Elizabeth considered it an honor to relate to Mary. She saw her potential for greatness and was able to celebrate it.

JOURNAL ASSIGNMENT: As you pray today, ask Holy Spirit to show you any adjustments that need to be made in your connections. Write out your plan of change.

_____

_____

_____

_____

_____

_____

_____

_____

_____

_____

_____

_____

_____

_____

_____

_____

_____

_____

_____

_____

_____

_____

_____

_____

_____

_____

_____

_____

_____

_____

_____

_____

_____

_____

_____

IMPLEMENTATION: Write your declarations regarding healthy relationships, find examples of healthy relationships in the bible, and meditate on them throughout the day.

PRAYER:

Father, bless this reader with the inner ability to not only find those predestined to make their purpose leap, but also to embrace them. I pray healthy relationships, connections, and associations over their lives. I declare that they will be able to flourish where they have been planted in every area of their lives. Teach them what a healthy relationship looks like. Strengthen them to judge their relationships and make any needed adjustments. In Jesus' Name. Amen.

Day 14

Come Out of Survival Mode

> ""Therefore I tell you, stop being worried or anxious (perpetually uneasy, distracted) about your life, as to what you will eat or what you will drink; nor about your body, as to what you will wear. Is life not more than food, and the body more than clothing? Look at the birds of the air; they neither sow [seed] nor reap [the harvest] nor gather [the crops] into barns, and yet your heavenly Father keeps feeding them. Are you not worth much more than they?"
> —Matthew 6:25-26 AMP

Many have the testimony of survival. You survived (to continue to live or exist, especially despite danger or hardship), but now it is time to thrive (to grow vigorously; prosper; flourish). It is time to become better, not bitter. It is time to use our stumbling blocks as stepping-stones. It is time to position ourselves for the level of kingdom reigning that God has laid up for us.

I want to challenge you today to use what you have gone through to bring healing and deliverance to the lives of those God has called you to impact. Maximize the opportunity!

Survival mode has one always on guard and waiting on the next bad thing to happen. There is no real peace in survival mode because you are fearfully watching your back and covering your stuff. You allow torment and torture to plague your mind and thoughts. You make desperate and unwise decisions based on your emotions.

When we begin to thrive, we see our God-ordained victory place. We rest in God's inner presence that empowers us to prosper continually. When we start to thrive, we set roots. We make commitments that better our lives. We find ourselves conquering giants and reigning as kings and priests in the earth realm.

JOURNAL ASSIGNMENT: Are you surviving or thriving? Do a self- check and write the areas you are merely surviving. Write out a plan of change.

_____

_____

_____

_____

_____

_____

_____

_____

_____

_____

_____

_____

_____

_____

_____

_____

_____

IMPLEMENTATION: Write your declarations regarding thriving in the kingdom in the bible and meditate on them throughout the day.

PRAYER:

I declare today that every decision you make will no longer be based on a survivor's mentality and that you will no longer operate with the mentality of those who merely thrive! I release the grace of God, the wisdom of God, and declare that you trust in The Lord! You will not make hasty decisions based on your fears and emotions, but you will truly wait on The Lord! I prophesy that you have come into your season of a mature trust that says, "I won't move until God speaks."

I declare that your season of trusting man more than you trust God is over! You will — from this day forward — trust in The Lord with all your heart, leaning not to your own understanding! You will acknowledge Him in all things knowing that He will direct, lead, and guide you. In Jesus' Name!

Day 15

Identify Those Who Are for You!

> "And he answered, Fear not: for they that be with us are more than they that be with them. And Elisha prayed, and said, Lord, I pray thee, open his eyes, that he may see. And the Lord opened the eyes of the young man; and he saw: and, behold, the mountain was full of horses and chariots of fire round about Elisha." —2 Kings 6:16-17

I *say this often because* I know the joy, freedom, and inspiration that comes with it! We waste too much time dumbing down, altering our personalities, and minimizing our dreams so that we will fit into places God never intended for us! You have hung around the chickens (those with coop mentalities that live limited lives and want you to be happy in their small dwelling) long enough. The Eagle in you has outgrown the coop! It is time to fly higher, dream bigger, and expect greater!

Perhaps your perspective of yourself is lower than it should be. You cannot hang around chickens (people with a coop mentality that refuse to make the necessary changes in their lives and are stuck and want you to remain stuck) and expect to SOAR.

Stop dumbing down the anointing to fit in. Stop wasting valuable time trying to convince insignificant ppl of what

God is doing in your life. Value your pearls. Find worth and value in yourself, and others will follow. Step out! Run Out! Get Out! Find those who are for you!

JOURNAL ASSIGNMENT: In what ways are you allowing the opinions of others to minimize your self-perspective? Have you been hanging around chickens or eagles? Make a conscious decision to value your pearls.

_____

_____

_____

_____

_____

_____

_____

_____

_____

_____

_____

_____

_____

_____

_____

_____

_____

_____

_____

_____

_____

_____

_____

_____

_____

_____

_____

_____

_____

_____

_____

_____

IMPLEMENTATION: Find Scriptures on your value, meditate on them, and write out your declarations for today.

PRAYER:

I declare strength today to boldly embrace the will of God for your life! I decree you will find unexplainable peace in your decision! I prophesy that there are more for you than against you! In Jesus' Name. Amen.

Day 16

Expect!

"Keep on asking and it will be given you; keep on seeking and you will find; keep on knocking [reverently] and [the door] will be opened to you. For everyone who keeps on asking receives; and he who keeps on seeking finds; and to him who keeps on knocking, [the door] will be opened."

—Matthew 7:7-8 AMP

G *ood Morning! The level* of expectancy you approach this day with determines the level of manifestation. Remember, God supplies on demand!

Enter this day with a level of expectation that demands manifestation! Face this day with a depth of expectation that brings a depth of manifestation that transcends every level of limitation on your life because expectation breaks barriers. Expectation defies the laws of limitation we have somehow adapted to while on this earth. Remember! We are not of this world. We only live in it.

The woman whose expectation was an acquittal, visited the home of the judge daily (Luke 18:5). She expected change. Her expectation caused the judge to see her acquittal as a means of peace for him. When is the last time your expectation shifted the axis of your purpose?

You are waiting on God, and God is waiting on you! You are waiting on God to bless you, and He already has! It is time out for merely hoping and believing. Expect the manifestation of the Word of God over every area of your life.

JOURNAL ASSIGNMENT: In what ways have you not been expecting God to move? Have you somehow settled for the doctor's report, thus negating the power of your healing?

_____

_____

_____

_____

_____

_____

_____

_____

_____

_____

_____

_____

_____

_____

_____

_____

_____

_____

_____

_____

_____

_____

_____

_____

_____

IMPLEMENTATION: Find and study Scriptures on expecting God to perform His Word, meditate on them, and write your declarations!!

PRAYER:

Father God, in the name above all names (Jesus), I pray for this your vessel. I declare that their expectation of Your Word is being multiplied and intensified! I decree that you are strengthening their faith in your Word. I declare that they are expecting healing, deliverance, and breakthrough. Stir up their hope in Your Word again. May they expect Your power and glory to manifest daily in their lives.

They are expecting windfalls, supernatural increase, and overflow. Their expectation has not been cut-off but heightened like never! In Jesus' Name. Amen.

Day 17

Judge Your Times and Seasons

"And of the children of Issachar, which were men that had understanding of the times, to know what Israel ought to do; the heads of them were two hundred; and all their brethren were at their commandment."

—1 Chronicles 12:32

If we are to fully experience our priestly places here on earth, we must possess the inner ability to judge our times and seasons. Ecclesiastes 3:1 states that "To everything there is a season, and a time to every purpose under the heaven:" We must connect with God in a deeper more intimate way in order to effectively discern our timing according to His plan and purpose for our lives. If not, we will find ourselves warring when we should be resting. We will find ourselves mourning when we should be rejoicing. We will find ourselves bitter when we should be better!

The sons of Issachar were so connected with God that their wisdom and insight led to a mighty nation. They embraced a woman judge (Deborah) when it was not accepted. They supported David before he became king. Their nation depended on their wisdom and judgment regarding times and seasons.

JOURNAL ASSIGNMENT: Write those areas where your discernment can improve and purpose in your heart to get closer to God to perfect those areas.

_____

_____

_____

_____

_____

_____

_____

_____

_____

_____

_____

_____

_____

_____

_____

_____

_____

_____

_____

_____

_____

_____

_____

_____

_____

_____

_____

_____

_____

_____

_____

IMPLEMENTATION: Find Scriptures on times and seasons. Make your declarations. Meditate on those Scriptures throughout the day.

PRAYER:

I declare that you operate under the anointing of the sons of Issachar and that you can judge your times and seasons. You are moving with the heartbeat of God in every area of our life. You are not behind Him or before Him, but you are in sync with His will and purpose for your life in this hour. In Jesus' Name. Amen.

Day 18

Die!

> "For where a testament is, there must also of necessity be the death of the testator. For a testament is of force after men are dead: otherwise it is of no strength at all while the testator liveth." —Hebrews 9:16-17

At some point, we must make a conscious decision to die so that Christ may dwell in us richly and totally. The death process may not feel good to our flesh, but it is good for our spiritual maturity. We must take control of our feelings and emotions.

Think naturally of a dead person lying in a coffin. If you talk rudely to them, what is their response? If you lie on them, what is their response? If you pinch them, what is their response? Absolutely nothing!

When we die to ourselves, we do not get offended. We do not get our feelings hurt. We do not get mad. We do, however, learn that these are all opportunities that we are presented with daily and make a conscious decision to live our lives according to the requirements of the Lord.

JOURNAL ASSIGNMENT: What are the hindrances to your death process? What makes you angry? What hurts your feelings? Write them down and a plan to come out of them.

_____

_____

_____

_____

_____

_____

_____

_____

_____

_____

_____

_____

_____

_____

_____

_____

_____

_____

_____

_____

_____

_____

_____

_____

_____

_____

_____

_____

_____

_____

_____

_____

_____

_____

_____

IMPLEMENTATION: Find Scriptures on the works of the flesh and make declarations regarding your life. Meditate on these Scriptures and your plan of change.

PRAYER:

Father, in the name of Jesus, I choose to die that You may reign in every area of my life. Deal with areas in my life that are hindrances to my death process. Heal every broken area that continues to cause me to revert to the places of comfort and complacency. This day, I die to my feelings and emotions. I die to what I think or feel. I die that You might live in and through me. In Jesus' Name. Amen.

Remember Lot's Wife!

"Remember [what happened to] Lot's wife [when she looked back]! Whoever seeks to save his life will [eventually] lose it [through death], and whoever loses his life [in this world] will keep it [from the consequences of sin and separation from God]." —Luke 17:32-33 AMP

In order to maintain your priestly place, you cannot look back. God told Lot to get his wife out of Sodom because of the destruction that was coming. His wife, however, could not let go. Perhaps it was her love for her family. Maybe it was the level of success she had obtained. It possibly could have been the fact that she was comfortable in Sodom.

This woman was destined to be a movement. However, her inability to embrace God's decision for her life, caused her to be a monument. Make a conscious decision to trust God and follow His path.

Beloved, when the Father begins to stretch you beyond your comfort zone, He desires to enlarge you. He sees your potential and knows the extent of the greatness He has invested in you. The worst thing you can do is retreat, look back, or revert to the place that no longer has the capacity to house you. Many are stuck between two levels (too big for where you were yet fearful of where you should be). Confront your fears! Trust God!

JOURNAL ASSIGNMENT: Write down any areas you feel a draw back. Write down the ways you are subtly looking back to people, relationships, habits, or even comfort places. Write out your plan of change.

_____

_____

_____

_____

_____

_____

_____

_____

_____

_____

_____

_____

_____

_____

_____

_____

_____

_____

_____

_____

_____

_____

_____

_____

_____

_____

_____

_____

_____

IMPLEMENTATION: Write out declarations regarding not looking back or reverting. Find and meditate on Scriptures of following God's plan for your life.

PRAYER:

Father, deal with any and everything in me that has the potential to rob me of my divine purpose. Show me the areas where I am reverting in my thinking. Show me the relationships that are not healthy for my forward momentum. Deal with the habits that I tend to find comfort in. Give me the strength and courage to face them. I want to be all You intended. In Jesus' Name. Amen.

Day 20

Stay Positioned!

> "And Deborah, a prophetess, the wife of Lapidoth, she judged
> Israel at that time. And she dwelt under the palm tree of
> Deborah between Ramah and Beth-el in mount Ephraim:
> and the children of Israel came up to her for judgment."
> —Judges 4:4-5

The younger I get; I realize that positioning is *everything.* Life happens. We are faced with situations and circumstances that can potentially rob us of our divine position with God. How we govern ourselves during these times determines our strength, persistence, and longevity.

I love the above passage that describes the posture of a woman of strength, stature, and governmental order. Deborah was a judge. She held an especially important position naturally, but her spiritual posture was what allowed her to do all that was expected of her. In this day and time, many of us wear many hats. Our lives demand a lot from us, and if we are not mindful of our posture, we can become overwhelmed, mentally exasperated, and depleted of our strength.

Deborah dwelt Under the palm trees (Wisdom) between Ramah (Peace) and Bethel (Presence of God). Wisdom covered and led her. She was not moved and overwhelmed emotionally. She rested between the peace and presence of God. Beloved, we must take this mindset when faced with seemingly impossible situations, overwhelming circumstances, and the daily cares of this world. Make a conscious decision to stay positioned!

JOURNAL ASSIGNMENT: Write down where you are positioned. Make a conscious decision to make any needed changes.

_____

_____

_____

_____

_____

_____

_____

_____

_____

_____

_____

_____

_____

_____

_____

_____

_____

_____

_____

_____

_____

_____

_____

_____

_____

_____

_____

_____

_____

_____

_____

IMPLEMENTATION: Meditate on the Position of Deborah throughout the day.

PRAYER

Father, life happens. I am often faced with issues that have the potential to rob me of my positioning with You. Help me to be governed by Your wisdom, and rest between Your perfect peace and Your presence. I need You more now than ever before. Lead me. Guide me. Cover and protect me, in Jesus' name.

Day 21

Open Your Mouth!

"Thou shalt also decree a thing, and it shall be established unto thee: and the light shall shine upon thy ways."

—Job 22:28

Y*ou were created to* reign as a King in the earth realm; a rich and powerful inheritance has been laid up for you. However, if you do not put a demand on it and settle for what manifests, you are living beneath your kingdom privileges.

Within you is an awesome inherent ability to shift atmospheres, shift your purpose, and call in the manifestation of your prophetic destiny. Unfortunately, many are stuck in cycles of failure, defeat, and are discontented — simply because they will not open their mouths.

When you are truly fed-up with lack, you pursue your increase. When you are tired of sickness invading your family, you begin to prophesy healing. Once you realize the authority in your mouth, things begin to shift and realign.

When it is your time, everything must line up with the will of the Lord for your life! Some of you are not experiencing that season of manifestation because you are not putting a demand on it! If you know it's your time, open your mouth and put a demand on the manifestation!

JOURNAL ASSIGNMENT: Write out the areas you know there is little or no manifestation of your kingdom authority. Write declarations and expect shift and change.

_____

_____

_____

_____

_____

_____

_____

_____

_____

_____

_____

_____

_____

_____

_____

_____

_____

_____

_____

_____

_____

_____

_____

_____

_____

_____

_____

_____

_____

_____

_____

_____

_____

_____

_____

IMPLEMENTATION: Read your declarations aloud seven times today.

PRAYER:

Father, in the name of Jesus, I decree that this person is breaking out of religious holding patterns and cycles of failure and defeat. I declare a greater determination to see the manifestation of Your Word in their lives. Increase their strength and ability to believe You for the impossible over every area of their lives. In Jesus' Name. Amen.

Conclusion

Kingdom Dominion is accessible and was given thousands of years ago because of the redemptive work of our Lord and Savior Jesus Christ. The keys to death, hell, and the grave were placed in your hands the day you gave your life to Christ. It makes no sense to cry for something you already have in your possession.

When life becomes difficult, pull out your keys. When you are faced with sickness, pull out your keys. Dig deeper into the Word of God, and change is inevitable.

Through the implementation of the wisdom strategies I have shared, you are now empowered to face each season of your life, expecting victory. I pray that your perception has been adjusted, and you are now ready to see life through the many promises in the book of Scriptures (Bible). Congratulations! You have just completed a milestone. For the past twenty days, you have maintained kingdom thoughts. You have created a habit. I encourage you to continue. Now, walk in your Kingdom Dominion.

www.ingramcontent.com/pod-product-compliance
Lightning Source LLC
LaVergne TN
LVHW051813080426
835513LV00017B/1938